The Campus History Series

California State University, Northridge

Following recommendations by the Regents of the University of California and the State Board of Education, the Donahoe Higher Education Act of 1960 brought San Fernando Valley State College (SFVSC) and other California state colleges together into one system. In June 1972, SFVSC joined the California State University system. In this photograph, campus president James Cleary monitors the installation of new signage on the Administration Building. (Courtesy of California State University, Northridge.)

On the Cover: SFVSC yell leaders are in formation in the parking lot at Woody's Smorgasburger around 1965. With locations on Reseda and Devonshire Boulevards, "Uncle Woody" of Woody's Smorgasburger advertised numerous popular "hootenanys" or "hoots" in the *Daily Sundial*, to which SFVSC students were invited to bring their own homemade instruments. (Courtesy of California State University, Northridge.)

Cover Background: Famed modernist architect Richard Neutra designed the SFVSC fine arts building. The structure was completed in 1960 but sustained heavy damage in the 1994 Northridge Earthquake, which resulted in the destabilization of toxic materials used at the time of the building's construction. As a result, it was demolished and replaced. (Courtesy of California State University, Northridge.)

The Campus History Series

CALIFORNIA STATE UNIVERSITY, NORTHRIDGE

ELLEN JAROSZ AND STEPHEN KUTAY

ARCADIA PUBLISHING

ISBN 978-1-4671-2995-4

Published by Arcadia Publishing
Charleston, South Carolina

Printed in the United States of America

Library of Congress Control Number: 2018944556

For all general information, please contact Arcadia Publishing:
Telephone 843-853-2070
Fax 843-853-0044
E-mail sales@arcadiapublishing.com
For customer service and orders:
Toll-Free 1-888-313-2665

Visit us on the Internet at www.arcadiapublishing.com

To the CSUN campus community,
especially students past, present, and future.

Contents

Acknowledgments

Since the founding of California State University, Northridge (CSUN), untold numbers of faculty, staff, students, and others have contributed their photographs, documents, and other resources to the University Archives. Thus they have created a documentary record of campus history and the experiences of individuals who worked and attended school here. While many of these individuals are unknown to us, our task would have been impossible without them. Numerous individuals across CSUN's campus and in the Oviatt Library provided support, encouragement, and assistance throughout the creation of this book, especially Jeff Noblitt, Shelley Hadvina, Rick Evans, and Oviatt Library dean Mark Stover. We also wish to extend heartfelt thanks to everyone in Special Collections and Archives, especially April Feldman, Mallory Furnier, and Julieta Garcia, who helped us track down difficult-to-find names, confirm locations, approximate dates, and proof our text, and contributed to the project in other immeasurable ways. Finally, we would be remiss if we did not thank our editor at Arcadia Publishing, Caroline Anderson.

Omissions are inevitable in a campus history of any form. We wrote for a general audience rather than trying to create a comprehensive and complete history. We selected historical images from archival holdings in CSUN's Special Collections and Archives. Though there are gaps, we hope these images will serve as windows to the past, reminding alumni of their time on campus and presenting current students, faculty, and staff with insights into the experiences of their predecessors. In conducting research, we relied heavily on issues of the *Daily Sundial*, stories in *CSUN Today*, various campus websites, and the contents of John Broesamle's 1993 campus history *Suddenly a Giant*.

All images in this book were graciously provided by California State University, Northridge. They are from the University Archives Photograph Collection unless otherwise noted. While many photographers are unknown to us, we would like to credit those we do know, including Virgil Heliker, Bill Ripple, and especially Lee Choo, who also graciously provided us access to many recent photographs of the campus.

INTRODUCTION

Established in the booming post–World War II period, CSUN is a young university by most measures. Over the short decades of its existence, it has rapidly grown into one of the largest universities in the nation. Today, hundreds of thousands of alumni hold degrees in myriad fields of study, numbers that spectacularly exceed the expectations of many early administrators and faculty members.

Shortly after California's state legislature chose a location east of downtown Los Angeles for the recently founded Los Angeles State College (LASC) campus, it authorized acquisition of an additional 160 acres for a satellite site in the San Fernando Valley. LASC president Howard McDonald and business manager Warner Masters soon began searching for potential sites in the largely undeveloped valley that could serve as home to the satellite campus. While numerous options were considered, the location was ultimately finalized when the City of Los Angeles traded 10 acres now occupied by the University Student Union (USU) for 10 acres in another valley location.

With LASC less than a decade old itself, the early development of its San Fernando Valley campus mirrored its own in many respects. Construction planning, curriculum development, and more occurred at both campuses simultaneously. President McDonald appointed Delmar Oviatt, chair of the Division of Education at LASC, to be dean of the valley campus in 1955. Valley classes taught by LASC faculty started in September of that year at San Fernando High School. In the absence of a campus bookstore, Oviatt reportedly sold required books and other texts to students from his car. A few months later, a ground-breaking ceremony was held at the valley campus site on January 4, 1956, in a patch of land recently divested of banana squash. Days later, construction of temporary buildings began in earnest.

From 1955 to 1958, the San Fernando Valley campus used LASC's curriculum and course catalog. There was no campus library, and Oviatt himself stamped every student registration card. Faculty who would teach exclusively at the valley campus were selected in 1956, primarily from LASC's existing faculty. In early 1957, a bill was introduced in the state legislature to establish the independent San Fernando Valley State College (SFVSC). Both houses of congress passed the measure, and it was signed by Gov. Goodwin Knight in July of that year. LASC's San Fernando Valley campus officially became San Fernando Valley State College one year later, on July 1, 1958.

Surrounded by orange groves and horse farms, early faculty described the new campus as small, rural, and charming, but those descriptors would not apply for long. In the late 1960s, just 10 years after the founding of SFVSC, the wave of student activism on campuses across the United States and around the world had significant impact here, as members of the Black Student Union (BSU), Students for a Democratic Society (SDS), United Mexican American Students (UMAS), and others engaged in demonstrations, sit-ins, occupations, and other acts of civil disobedience while pushing for higher enrollment of students from underserved communities, more courses on issues important to those communities, and the end of the Vietnam War and many of the tactics employed by the federal government in fighting it. Los Angeles Police Department (LAPD) officers were on campus repeatedly in plain clothes and in riot gear.

Matters came to a head on November 4, 1968, when black student athletes, BSU members, and other students seized the sixth floor of the Administration Building, demanding reform. From this student-led effort came the establishment of the departments of pan African (now Africana) and Mexican American (now Chicana/o) studies in 1969, which increased support and funding for the Educational Opportunities Program and students from underserved communities. In the coming decades, numerous other ethnic and area studies programs were established on campus, including American Indian studies, Asian American studies, Central American studies, gender and women's studies, Jewish studies, queer studies, and more. Of equal significance was the emergence of a campus culture where students are deeply invested in the form and structure of their own educations and engage in activism on campus and more broadly.

Following these years of tumult, the 1970s and 1980s saw significant administrative changes, most notably as SFVSC joined the new California State University system as California State University, Northridge on June 1, 1972. The following year, a new and iconic campus library was completed and named for founding campus administrator Delmar Oviatt, who had passed away the year before. This period also saw the campus's first attempts at reforming general education requirements. While these efforts at many other universities around the United States were mired in controversy and conflict, at CSUN, a new cross-cultural studies requirement was implemented without challenge. With the San Fernando Valley's accelerating residential development over these years, the campus also increasingly served as a hub for the surrounding community.

On January 17, 1994, a 6.7-magnitude earthquake struck the San Fernando Valley, killing 72 people. The quake was catastrophic, resulting in more than $300 million in damages on campus alone. Under president Blenda Wilson's leadership, faculty, staff, and students pulled together in the earthquake's immediate aftermath and stunningly opened the campus for classes only two weeks after the spring semester's originally planned start date. Faculty and administrators worked out of tents, and classes were taught in trailers and other temporary structures as emergency and construction crews began the slow process of rebuilding. CSUN grew into its role as a resource for the surrounding community as it recovered from the devastation, providing a forum for national, state, and local dignitaries to offer assistance, provide encouragement, and more generally support local efforts.

Today, CSUN is a true people's university. While it differs in many respects from the ambitions of the earliest faculty and administrators, it has developed a unique and proud character. In some ways, the student body has grown more similar to that of other universities, but in others, it stands out. Many CSUN students are the first in their families to go to college. Others are immigrants or the children of immigrants. Also a point of distinction for the campus, CSUN stands out in that it was students who raised the campus's profile in the national arena. Faculty largely recognize and value their engagement and contributions and take pride in working to provide a quality, affordable education. CSUN has faced unique challenges and opportunities, in part due to its rapid growth into one of the largest universities in the country. Today, it is enormously successful in providing accessible higher education to residents of the San Fernando Valley, Los Angeles, and beyond.

One

Founding and Growth 1955–1965

California State University, Northridge started as many other institutions in the San Fernando Valley did, with trees cleared and foundations poured at sites that were once orange, lemon, and avocado groves. While it passed its first years as the San Fernando Valley campus of Los Angeles State College, it became San Fernando Valley State College before the fall 1958 term. The student body and faculty cohort were quite small in comparison with today but quickly developed a sense of community.

As the number of faculty and students almost immediately began to grow, so did the campus itself. Pres. Ralph Prator oversaw a number of construction projects in the college's early years, resulting in the opening of several buildings in rapid succession. These included the first cafeteria, the speech-drama building, the Neutra-designed fine arts building, the original library, the natural science buildings, the music building, the Sierra complex, and Monterey Hall, the college's first dormitory. Rapid growth meant that the campus community often strained the capacity of new infrastructure even as it was built, with early students engaging in endless tricks to find parking spots. Despite the push for new buildings and other infrastructure, campus administrators preserved one of the original orange groves in honor of the region's agricultural history.

Even in the campus's earliest years, students organized and participated in many of the typical trappings of college life. Homecoming parades ran down Reseda Boulevard, yell leaders led cheers at athletic and other events, students participated in coed tugs-of-war, incoming freshmen participated in freshman sports nights, and an annual all-college picnic brought students, faculty, and administrators together to socialize. The campus radio station was approved in 1962 and began broadcasting the following year. In addition to these student-focused activities, the campus also hosted visits from numerous national politicians, including Nelson Rockefeller, William F. Buckley Jr., and Lyndon Johnson.

In 1952, Baldwin Hills was selected as the site for a satellite campus of Los Angeles State College. However, a meeting at the famous Brown Derby restaurant on Wilshire Boulevard gave valley leaders, led by Assemblyman Julian Beck, a chance to woo legislators into reconsidering their decision in favor of the booming businesses and population of the San Fernando Valley. At 2:00 p.m. on January 4, 1956, a crowd of more than 500 students and faculty gathered at Nordhoff Street and Zelzah Avenue in Northridge with state and California state college officials to break ground for the San Fernando Valley campus of LASC. Pictured from left to right are Patricia Kilpatrick, 1955–1956 LASC homecoming queen; Howard McDonald, Los Angeles State College president; Goodwin Knight, governor of California; and Roy E. Simpson, California superintendent of public instruction.

A squash field once occupied the site of the San Fernando Valley campus of LASC. Photographed shortly after it was purchased in 1955 but before construction began in January 1956, the field features a newly installed sign reading "State Property: Any person removing or molesting same will be prosecuted to the full extent of the law, Department of Public Works."

The erection of this billboard was described in the *Sundial*'s October 3, 1957, issue. From left to right are Howard McDonald, LASC president; Delmar Oviatt, dean of the San Fernando Valley campus; Ken Kearsley, Associated Students (AS) vice president; and Robert Lawrence, coordinator of student activities. The billboard was on the corner of Nordhoff Street and Zelzah Avenue.

As a satellite campus of LASC, the San Fernando Valley campus's faculty, nearly all of whom are pictured here, were modestly numbered. From left to right are (first row) Mervyn Soyster, Mr. McIntyre, Max [Klinger?], Prudence Bostwick, Betty Brady, unidentified, Jack Kudena, and Ruth Roche; (second row) Dr. John Gowan, Dr. Cliff Winn, and unidentified.

Students and administrators at the San Fernando Valley campus of LASC join to raise the flag over temporary buildings covered in wet paint as classes start on September 24, 1956. After the flag's raising, Associated Students president Ben Rude accepted a ceremonial presentation of the library's first book as the student body, numbering 1,500, officially began the semester.

This aerial view from 1956 shows a campus just beginning to take shape in the San Fernando Valley. Temporary buildings served as classrooms to the 135 freshmen registered in 1957, as seen at center, facing west at the intersection of Nordhoff Street and Zelzah Avenue. At this time, the surrounding area was still dominated by groves of oranges among newly constructed tract homes.

Associated Students welcomed students to the San Fernando Valley campus in this cartoon, printed in the second issue of the student newspaper, now called *Daily Sundial*. The first issue ran with a question mark in place of a title, and the second issue ran with the title *What's in a Name?* While the title changed several more times over the course of the term, by the following fall, it was the now-familiar *Sundial*.

As president of Bakersfield College in the 1950s, Ralph Prator helped lead the construction of a new campus for that college. The experience made him uniquely qualified to serve in the same capacity for the newly designated state college in Northridge. Much of his time during the early years in Northridge was spent pressing city and state officials for more land to accommodate immediate and steady increases in enrollment. Indeed, during his tenure, enrollment levels surged by over 450 percent from 3,500 to 16,000 students. Prator oversaw the construction of many of the campus's core buildings, including the original library (later called the South Library). After 10 years, Prator resigned in 1968 amid rising racial tensions across California and the nation. This c. 1958 portrait was taken shortly after he assumed his post as the first president of SFVSC.

Faculty members pose at an early commencement ceremony held on campus. The first commencement ceremony for SFVSC students was in 1958, with exercises for just over 100 graduates held at the Hollywood Bowl. In 1959, commencement exercises were moved to campus, where they were held on a football field. Graduating classes grew rapidly in the early years, with 1,155 graduating in 1964.

For many years, SFVSC had its own big band. The Faculty and Staff Dance Band is seen here performing at the State Employees Dinner Dance on November 18, 1961, in the then-new cafeteria. On the photograph's back, photographer Virgil Heliker noted the absence of trombonist Dr. Addie Klotz, who was head of the health department. Humorously, the musicians who do appear in the image are not identified.

Judge Julian Beck is pictured with SFVSC president Ralph Prator and his wife, Lois, around 1960 as they roll down Reseda Boulevard in a convertible Cadillac as part of the homecoming parade. Beck was instrumental in founding SFVSC as coauthor of the resolution permitting its construction. He continued to fill an influential role at the college, serving multiple terms as the chairman of the SFVSC Advisory Board after its inception in 1958.

Members of the SFVSC Advisory Board in 1958 included community leaders who helped the college gain its independence from LASC. The board included, from left to right, (first row) Judge Julian Beck, Mrs. Owen, and Dr. Ralph Prator; (second row) Ferdinand Mendenhall of the *Daily News*, philanthropist Russell Quisenberry, Sam Hoffman, Dr. Marshall, and Nathan Freedman of the Northridge Chamber of Commerce.

When a new cafeteria opened in 1961, Associated Students converted the original cafeteria space into a temporary student union. Furnished with modern and comfortable sofas and chairs, it was renamed the Bull Ring and included a snack bar, game room, and television room. The snack bar opened before the rest of the building as a convenience to students who were unable to visit the new cafeteria across campus between classes.

By 1961, the campus had largely lost its agricultural character, and new buildings near Etiwanda Avenue, Nordhoff Street, and Lindley Avenue formed a new perimeter. This aerial photograph shows the original library (center), fine arts (center left), cafeteria, natural science (center right), speech-drama (bottom left), and music (center bottom) buildings, as well as the Monterey Hall dormitory (far right). At top is Devonshire Downs, a racing track removed decades later to develop North Campus.

Students anxiously waited as workers rushed to complete a new cafeteria by the January 3, 1960, deadline. The desperately needed $1.2-million cafeteria featured an 1,800-seat dining room and 200-person banquet room. Among the amenities were three 300-gallon kettle steamers, an electric potato peeler, and a conveyor-belt-driven dishwasher capable of cleaning 200 dishes per hour.

The new cafeteria opened in 1961 and served as many as 2,400 students per day in its first week, nearly twice as many as the original cafeteria. A separate seating area was reserved for faculty and staff. Students were asked to bus their own tables, which required that they bring their dishes to the heavy-duty conveyor-belt dishwasher.

The speech-drama building, now called Nordhoff Hall, was built by the Steed Bros. Construction Co. of Alhambra, California. The building officially opened on March 7, 1961, with three weeks of special events held to mark the occasion. The first was a special lecture, "The Craftsmanship of Shakespeare's *Othello*," by English professor Dr. Mitchell Marcus. The final event was a performance of the very same play in the new theater.

Sierra Tower was completed in 1963. As the tallest building at SFVSC, it made a grand profile in addition to connecting Sierra Hall North (now Jerome Richfield Hall) and Sierra Hall South (now Sierra Hall). Campus administrators were bracing for an influx of students. The newly paved street, which would later be converted for foot traffic and christened Matador Walk, would accommodate numerous commuters from the San Fernando Valley and beyond.

The campus's continuing development can be seen in this 1963 aerial photograph. By then, the large Sierra Hall complex (center left), Administration Building (upper center left), engineering building (upper center), and physical science buildings (upper center right) had been completed. The number of available parking spaces was also increased (bottom left), but one of the original orange groves was preserved (bottom right).

Though the Sierra complex was completed in 1963, the tower remained uninhabited until the spring 1964 semester. Functional electricity in the building inspired this welcome to students, staff, and faculty: lighted windows spell "VSC" on floors four through eight. Later that year, the campus initials were replaced with an expletive in response to John F. Kennedy's assassination, resulting in the building being temporarily closed.

With enrollment growing at Valley State, services such as parking were almost immediately strained. In 1964, the college sold 2,800 parking decals for 1,582 parking spaces. Desperate students with and without permits reportedly came up with creative ways to find parking spots, sometimes gaming the system by constructing counterfeit gate keys, trading and sharing keys, and entering the lot by driving through the orange grove rather than using the official entrance. Students, faculty, and other commuters who parked in unpaved fields and clearings near campus risked fines. The full lot shown here is a vast construction nestled within the valley landscape.

With news cameras in position, senator and Democratic vice presidential nominee Lyndon B. Johnson visited SFVSC on October 25, 1960. Accompanied by California governor Pat Brown and others, he arrived in dramatic fashion via a helicopter that landed and took off behind the library. Wearing his trademark Stetson, he greeted and addressed approximately 3,500 students, faculty, community members, and others at a rally in front of the library before signing autographs.

3,500 See Johnson Fly In, Talk, Greet Hosts

—Photo by Ed Murdock —Photo by Paul Dexler —Photo by Paul Dexler

Johnson Denounces Nixon, Calls Platform Stagnant

VALLEY STATE SUNDIAL

3,500 Hear Return Told of 'Old Nixon'

Some attendees at vice presidential nominee Johnson's rally carried signs supporting other candidates in the 1960 presidential race or commenting on controversial issues relevant in the nation at the time. In his remarks, Johnson denounced Richard Nixon and the Republican party's platform, calling the platform "stagnant" and Nixon a "desperate man."

After the 1964 Oregon primary, New York governor Nelson Rockefeller visited SFVSC. Ralph Prator introduced the Republican candidate to a crowd of approximately 6,000 gathered beside the library, later renamed the South Library. Rockefeller's appearance was sponsored by the college Republican Club. He ultimately lost the nomination to Barry Goldwater, who was defeated by Johnson in the general election.

In December 1965, over 4,000 people crammed into the SFVSC gymnasium to witness a debate cosponsored by the Lectures and Concerts Committee, the Associated Valley Young Republicans, and the Valley State Young Republicans. Conservative William F. Buckley Jr., host of the television show *Firing Line*, and liberal Louis Lomax, a highly regarded African American journalist who hosted the *Louis E. Lomax Show*, debated the federal government's role in civil rights.

Established in 1962, the National Leadership Training Program developed critical interpreting, note taking, and tutoring services that helped increase the enrollment of deaf and hard-of-hearing students at SFVSC. Campus Services for the Deaf helped make it one of the most accessible campuses in the nation for this underserved community. The campus completed an upgraded facility for the renamed National Center on Deafness, Jeanne M. Chisholm Hall (pictured), in 1989.

Upon approval by the Federal Communications Commission, SFVSC's radio station began broadcasting in November 1963 from the speech-drama department under the call letters KEDC at 88.5 on the FM dial. According to faculty supervisor Dr. Bertram (Bert) Barer, programming would consist of "good music, speeches, panel discussions, and news." In addition to broadcast majors, all students were welcome to participate in the programming. Initially, the station broadcast five days a week between 4:00 and 8:00 p.m. Today, the award-winning station operates under the call letters KCSN and continues to provide exemplary student and professional programming.

Completed in the mid-1960s on a site that had been covered by orange trees, the Administration Building originally housed all campus administrative offices, including the president's office, the placement bureau, the registration office, admissions, and the registrar, among others. The building has been known successively as the Student Services Building and Bayramian Hall, and still houses multiple student services departments.

A popular student activity in the campus's early years, men's, women's, and coed tug-of-war competitions were a feature of numerous events organized throughout the academic year, including annual All-College Picnics, the Frosh-Soph Competition, Freshman Sports Nights, and more. Other popular campus activities included softball and trivia games organized between students and faculty, capture-the-flag games between teams of upper- and lowerclassmen, and dances.

Two

Students Take the Lead 1966–1972

SFVSC underwent dramatic and significant changes in the late 1960s and early 1970s. As the nation saw a rapid shift of social values and political consciousness, widespread conflict erupted between young people, especially students, and members of older generations who were often in positions of power. Political figures began visiting college campuses more frequently than they had previously, including SFVSC, which hosted visits by Hubert Humphrey, Robert F. Kennedy, and Eugene McCarthy, among others. The campus also saw an increased police presence over these years, with LAPD officials delivering intelligence reports to Delmar Oviatt about planned protest actions. Despite concerns expressed by faculty about mounting levels of violence between students and police, confrontations resulted in student arrests and other penalties.

While anti–Vietnam War sentiments were at the heart of some SFVSC protest actions, many students organized themselves around more local concerns. Chief among these were increasing access to higher education for students from diverse backgrounds and the creation of ethnic studies departments and programs to promote the awareness and advancement of underserved communities. Students presented a list of demands to campus administrators following a takeover of the Administration Building in late 1968, but tensions remained high as LAPD officers forcibly broke up student rallies and other protest actions through the early 1970s. While students of color started and led these movements, students and faculty from many backgrounds ultimately stood with members of such organizations as the BSU and UMAS.

Despite the tension and turmoil, the campus continued to grow over these years. Its infrastructure progressed with construction of new residence halls and a reflecting pool, the installation of public sculptures, and a new library. Students and faculty continued to attend classes and conduct research. A 1971 earthquake caused destruction across campus, though it was not as damaging as the one that would strike in 1994. In 1972, one of the most significant administrative changes in campus history occurred as San Fernando Valley State College joined the new California State University system, becoming California State University, Northridge.

In 1968, SFVSC experienced a surge in student political activity that drew numerous campaigning politicians interested in securing student votes to campus. On March 25, 1968, Democratic presidential candidate Robert F. Kennedy spoke to a crowd of 10,000 students and other spectators who were overwhelmingly energized by their opposition to the Vietnam War. In his address to the largest crowd yet seen at SFVSC, Kennedy lauded the tremendous spirit of youth and urged the nation to "throw away false hopes of military conquest in Vietnam." Supporters of Republican candidates Richard Nixon and Ronald Reagan could also be spotted in the crowd.

Students crowded the podium, climbed trees, and scaled buildings in order to get a good look at Robert F. Kennedy. His platform was largely built around social justice and civil rights issues, leading to the defeat of his strongest opponent, Eugene McCarthy, in the California primaries shortly after his visit to campus. In his address, Kennedy conceded that negotiations with the Viet Cong in North Vietnam would be required for any peaceful resolution to the Vietnam War. Given Kennedy's frequent criticism of the war, some in the audience were surprised by his admission that had he been drafted, he would have fought. He also addressed jobs, welfare, and support for a lowering of the voting age to 18, which was universally lauded by the crowd.

On the heels of Kennedy's successful visit, Eugene McCarthy, another candidate in the 1968 Democratic presidential primary, spoke to a crowd of 7,000 at SFVSC. With California's coveted electoral votes at stake, college campuses became a strategic priority for candidates seeking support from politically mobilized collegiate voters in the late 1960s. Despite campus polling favoring McCarthy, the crowd was several thousand fewer than expected.

In September 1966, Valley State received a visit from Vice Pres. Hubert Humphrey. By this time, students and others around the country were expressing great displeasure with US military involvement and practices in Southeast Asia, as evidenced by the antiwar sentiment expressed on signs held by some in the audience. Also seen are signs supporting gubernatorial candidate Pat Brown, who ultimately lost to Ronald Reagan.

Led by BSU members Jerome Walker, Archie Chatman, and Bill Burwell, SFVSC students sought to increase the number of enrolled black students on campus and create a curriculum for black studies. Eventually, the Educational Policies Committee signaled its willingness to hear program proposals for what was then termed "minority studies," resulting in new Africana and Chicana/o studies programs, with dozens of new courses.

Members of the BSU, SDS, and others famously took over the Administration Building in November 1968 in the immediate aftermath of a coach's assault on a student athlete, often called the November Fourth Incident. The following January, BSU members met with university administrators in the same building while LAPD officers used force to break up a student rally just outside.

After campus administrators nullified demands made by students in the aftermath of the November Fourth Incident, demonstrations became more frequent. By this time, some white students and faculty expressed solidarity with the BSU, joining them in protests. Delmar Oviatt was acting president on January 8, 1969, when over 300 students marched to the Administration Building and demanded to speak with him. Security personnel attempted to impede their progress, but some forced their way inside before the doors were locked. From the fifth floor, riot police who had been monitoring the previous days' protests came down to the lobby. Determined to enter the building, students heaved a heavy ashtray through the glass door, setting off an immediate backlash from the police.

275 ARRESTED

DAILY SUNDIAL

Vol. 13, No. 53 Valley State College Friday, January 10, 1969

llegal assembly' broken u

On the evening of January 8, 1969, English professors Wallace Graves and Marvin Klotz delivered a letter to acting president Oviatt that had been signed by 12 faculty members. The letter expressed concern about the risk of police violence during an open forum demonstration planned for the following day and recommended that classes be closed at noon so students could peacefully convene. Hours later, Oviatt received an LAPD intelligence report alleging that 2,000 agitators from black communities were expected to join the planned demonstration. He declared a state of emergency, further inflaming matters. The next day, 100 police officers arrested campus minister Rev. Tom Laswell, Mike Lee, and BSU president Archie Chatman. Students clasped arms as police systematically arrested 275 demonstrators, including Dr. Graves and seven other faculty members, in what was described by the LAPD press relations officer as "the most peaceful arrest in the history of the nation."

A free-form sculpture is seen here in front of the fine arts annex surrounded by the seasonal blossoms of ornamental pear trees. The three-dimensional forms were created by artist Jan Peter Stern, who donated them to the campus. Transportation and installation required trucks and booms to make the trip from Century City. Initially installed between the music and speech-drama buildings, the sculpture was moved to the fine arts building in 1970.

Around 1966, students and faculty at the National Center on Deafness test the speech indicator. According to Dr. Ray Jones, chairman of the Leadership Training Program in the Area of the Deaf, the device unlocked the telephone for deaf persons so they would be able to engage with a larger community of people and have increased vocational opportunities.

In 1968, the area southwest of the Administration Building, renamed Bayramian Hall in 2005, featured a reflecting pool. The sculpture in the pool, titled *Two Up, Two Down*, is a stainless steel kinetic work by artist George Rickey. The sculpture now resides in front of the Soraya, the performing arts center on campus.

Around 1966, spirited cheerleaders nearly spell out the initials for San Fernando Valley State College while perched on benches on the football field's sideline. School spirit was led by cheerleaders, yell leaders (most of whom were men), and the school marching band. In 1966–1967, the SFVSC football team experienced much success, keeping the spirit squads extra busy.

From San Fernando Valley State's earliest days, the campus hosted the annual summer Teenage Drama Workshop to expose youths to the dramatic arts. The workshops produced multiple productions each season. This popular and award-winning program has continued to flourish over the decades into what is now a six-week conservatory-style camp for 7th- to 12th-graders. In 1968, the workshop produced the musical *Rags to Riches* (below) and delivered an impressive 10 performances from July 11 through July 20. Above are two workshop participants in character (and dog costume).

SFVSC engineering majors received cash scholarships from Alcoa in 1967. From left to right, junior James Brier, senior Monte Richard, and senior Jan Smed receive $250 each with certificates presented by the dean of the School of Engineering, Dr. George T. Harness (right). Winners were selected from among a group of eligible students by the engineering faculty's Student Affairs Committee.

Fewer than three dozen black and Chicano students were enrolled at SFVSC in 1967. Grants provided by the federal Educational Opportunity Program (EOP) were offered to institutions to begin increasing the annual enrollment of underrepresented students, and in the fall of 1968, SFVSC established its local EOP, seen here in a meeting of the first cohort of EOP students.

The Northridge Hall residence building, on Zelzah Avenue, opened to student occupants in January 1967. It featured two three-story wings, one for women and one for men. Student residents could expect to pay $1,195 for a room shared with another student each academic year. Coeds in the women's wing of the new residence hall found time to socialize and study in the self-service beauty salon. The men's wing of the building featured a small gym. The first coeducational dormitory at SFVSC, Northridge Hall also included a pool, dining hall, and study room.

In a demonstration of his love for teaching, Alan Josefsberg takes time during summer break as the Palms Junior High School drama teacher to direct a production of *Pied Piper* for the 1970 Teenage Drama Workshop at SFVSC. This production marked Josefsberg's return to the workshop after having played the role of Burgomaster in the same play 12 years earlier, when he was himself an SFVSC student during the second annual Teenage Drama Workshop. The workshop was created to provide opportunities for local teenagers to participate in summer productions on campus. Josefsberg received his teaching credential from SFVSC in 1966.

By the fall of 1966, rapid growth in student enrollment was evident in the strain on existing student services and facilities at SFVSC. In this photograph, students wait in line to return and purchase books before the new term. According to bookstore manager William Holbrook, the lengthy line helped motivate students to expedite their selections and purchases. In an attempt to alleviate congestion in future semesters, Holbrook made plans in late September 1966 to add new wall-mounted shelves to the bookstore and change its layout. Going forward, he placed the required and recommended texts for the same course beside each other and moved cash registers to the sides rather than positioning them near the entrance. Finally, Holbrook added a rack that featured magazines ranging from *Mad* to *Mademoiselle*, as requested by many students.

From 1951 to 1972, the annual Pro Bowl, featuring NFL all-stars, was held at the Los Angeles Memorial Coliseum. On January 23, 1972, the SFVSC Matador Band entertained the audience of over 53,000 at halftime. Above, the band, players, and color guard are assembled for the national anthem, and below, the band and dance team perform for the crowd.

Science fiction author Ray Bradbury began his relationship with SFVSC on May 10, 1960, when he delivered a special lecture on campus titled "The Writing of Science Fiction." Over the coming decades, he would give similar lectures on campus. Bradbury also collaborated on publications produced by the Santa Susana Press, established in 1975 by library dean Norman Tanis. *The God in Science Fiction* was published by the press's facsimile series for CSUN's 20th anniversary, when Bradbury spoke at the University Student Union's Northridge Center. The press also published two additional works, *About Norman Corwin* (1979) and "The Last Good Kiss" (1984). Bradbury's support for the art of the book was further on display during a public printing of his poem "To Ireland." The poem was freshly printed on a press and autographed by the author in the library lobby as part of the CSUN Silver Anniversary festivities in 1983.

The razing of 10 trees and a track provided the scene for the ground breaking of a new campus library on May 19, 1971. Above, Pres. James Cleary is pictured with library dean Norman Tanis (far right). The new library, designed by architect Leo A. Daly, was built across from the original library, renamed the South Library after its completion. With a budget of $7.5 million, the building was opened to students weeks before its October 24, 1973, dedication to Dr. Delmar T. Oviatt. Seen below shortly after its completion, the iconic Oviatt Library sits atop a gently sloping hill on campus. In 1991, the structure was expanded as part of a second phase that added east and west wings.

At 6:00 a.m. on February 9, 1971, an earthquake in the foothills of the San Gabriel Mountains caused severe damage at SFVSC. In the original library, nearly a quarter-million books tumbled to the floor, piling up to five feet deep in some areas and blocking many walkways. Library officials closed the upper floors for several weeks in order to repair shelves and reorganize library collections, aided in their work by students and other volunteers from across campus. Other buildings on campus saw shattered windows, flooded classrooms, and more serious structural damage. Damage to just the engineering building, bookstore, Sierra Tower, and library resulted in a preliminary estimate for repairs at nearly $200,000.

Three

Developing Services and Programs 1973–1980

By the mid-1970s, dramatic confrontations between students, faculty, campus administration, and the LAPD had largely ceased. For the rest of the decade, CSUN president James Cleary presided over steady increases in the size of the student body and the further development and growth of numerous programs. Notably, students elected William Watkins as the first African American student body president in these years; he would become a longstanding member of the CSUN community. Outreach to and programs for young people in underserved communities expanded, with some colleges and departments establishing scholarship funds for students for the first time. Faculty research of increasingly high profile continued.

The physical appearance of the campus and its infrastructure also continued to grow and change, with several new buildings opening for use, most notably the Klotz Student Health Center. In addition to buildings, these years saw the installation of the multidimensional CSUN sculpture on Nordhoff Street and Zelzah Avenue, the establishment of the Santa Susana Press in the Oviatt Library, and the expansion of services in the counseling center on campus.

In addition to the typical rhythms of college life, the mid- and late 1970s also saw numerous high-profile visitors to campus. These included Cesar Chavez, who visited campus twice, once as an invited speaker and again to build support for a statewide ballot measure. World-renowned Spanish classical guitarist Andrés Segovia visited students and faculty in CSUN's acclaimed guitar program. Aaron Copland, one of the best-known composers of the 20th century, attended a music festival at CSUN where he conducted student musicians as they played his compositions.

The career of CSUN's second president, James Cleary, spanned an impressive 23 years, from 1969 to 1992. During his time at CSUN, Cleary provided important leadership through times of growth and social change. He presided over the change of the university's name and a 10,000-student increase in enrollment. He negotiated the difficult but critical development of the university's first ethnic studies programs, including Chicana/o studies and pan-African studies (later renamed Africana studies). The Cleary era was also marked by intensive construction, which included North Campus dormitories and athletic fields, as well as numerous additional phases to existing buildings. In 1986, the Exxon Education Foundation recognized President Cleary as one of the 100 most effective college presidents in the United States.

In 1972, a track and field installation was removed to make way for a new library to serve the growing campus. Seen here, phase one of the library is nearing completion. At upper left is Rincon Hall, later renamed University Apartments. This structure signaled shifting priorities in developing the North Campus for student housing and athletic facilities.

In 1958, the student health center was a single room in an off-campus bungalow run by two doctors and a nurse. Plans to build a larger health center stalled until a 1967 survey confirmed the need for student health centers in the California State College system. Construction of a new center was completed in 1976. The Addie L. Klotz Student Health Center now hosts over 30 doctors and nurses.

Standing over 7 feet tall and 31 feet wide, John Banks's unique three-dimensional design enables the sign to be read from angles 90 degrees apart. This west-facing view of the sculpture was captured in 1975 atop the base containing the university name. See page 62 to compare it with the north-facing view.

The CSUN sculpture created by student John Banks is at the corner of Nordhoff Street and Zelzah Avenue. Banks won a campus-wide competition amongst a total of six submitted designs. Banks is seen in 1975 hanging from the intricate rebar pattern that formed the letter *C*. A ceremony revealing the completed sculpture and sign took place on April 30, 1975, and featured commentary by Pres. James W. Cleary.

Early on, CSUN was recognized for its innovation in programs for the deaf. Led by director Dr. Ray Jones (left), a site was selected in 1979 for what would be called Jeanne M. Chisholm Hall in 1989. Home to the National Center on Deafness, Chisholm Hall was made possible in part by strong support of the San Fernando Valley Industrial Association (now Valley Industry and Commerce Association), represented by then-president Robert E. Gibson (right).

Norman Tanis, former dean of the Oviatt Library, operates a printers proof press made by the Paul Shniedewende Co. in the lobby of the Oviatt around 1975. It was one of three presses used in the production of broadsides and books published by the library's Santa Susana Press. Started by Tanis in 1973, some of its publications were collaborations with John Updike, Ray Bradbury, and art history professor Hans Burkhardt.

A.S. PRESIDENT

William Watkins elected

Watkins

Upper Division Senator William Watkins won one of the most controversial and tense elections in California State University, Northridge history.

Watkins, an A.S. senator for two years, finished ahead of opponent Jim Conran. Election results may be contested.

Voting results

WATKINS 1623
CONRAN 1306

News censorship

Over 7,000 issues of the Daily Sundial were stolen from their boxes Thursday morning. For complete details see page 2.

SUN DIAL

Vol. 17, No. 96
California State University, Northridge
Friday, May 4, 1973

DENIES MEMO

Buttitta--'not involved'

By RIP RENSE
Staff Writer

Associated Students Sports Information Director Joe Buttitta said he had "nothing to do" with the production or working of the controversial memo given to athletics department faculty which endorsed former A.S. presidential candidate Jim Conran.

Although the memo was labelled "from: Joe Buttitta and Jim Bird," Buttitta said he did not authorize Bird to use his name. Bird, an athletics graduate assistant has since apologized to Buttitta and said he used Buttitta's name to "add more weight" to the memo. (Buttitta is well known in the athletics department.)

In an official statement to A.S. Business Manager Ashok Dhingra, Buttitta said his only involvement with the memo occurred when Bird asked him Monday if he approved of "reminding" athletics department coaches and faculty of the impending runoff election. Buttitta said he told Bird "it probably would help." He made it clear his involvement ended there and said the first time he saw the memo was in the Sundial (Wednesday, May 2, page 1).

Buttitta had been pressured to resign by A.S. President Dennia Gai because of what Gai called "unethical conduct" and using A.S. facilities to distribute the memo. Although Buttitta denies any involvement with the memo's production Gai has not changed his stand.

The factor causing Gai to doubt Buttitta's word is a proposal made by board member Jim Bird on today's personnel board meeting agenda to change Buttitta's employer from Dhingra (A.S.) to Assistant Athletics Director Sam Winningham (the athletics department). Gai did not elaborate on this.

Dhingra hopes to complete his investigation of the matter in time for the meeting, scheduled for 11 a.m. in his office.

Bird wrote the memo and distributed it to athletic department faculty Tuesday. Administration and A.S. officials have called the memo "at least unethical," but none could find anything illegal about it. In essence, the memo asked athletics faculty to urge students to vote for Conran.

Although Bird is receiving one unit of faculty credit (to protect the school from state lawsuit if he is injured) and is being paid for coaching, he is not classified as a faculty member. It is illegal for faculty members to use school facilities to campaign for an A.S. candidate.

Court refuses to recognize election

The Associated Students Constitutional Court will not recognize the final voting results which were compiled Thursday night until defeated Senatorial candidate Corey Ingber's appeal against Jim Conran is heard, acting Chief Justice David Diaz announced.

The court resheduled its Thursday meeting to Monday night at 7 because Assistant Dean of Activities Dan Walters was unable to preside.

"The vote will be counted tonight and if they (the A.S. Constitutional Court) want to monkey around with the results they can do it all they want," Walters said Thursday.

The SFVSC student body elected Ben Rude as its first AS president in 1957. William Watkins became CSUN's first African American AS president in 1973 after winning a controversial runoff election. In the immediate aftermath, his opponent's supporters contested the results, attempted to impeach outgoing AS president Dennis Gai, and worked to censure director of elections Mark Bell. Ultimately, Watkins's tenure was the beginning of a long career in leadership on the campus. In 1981, twenty-five years after the first AS election, Susan Ettinger became the first woman AS president.

Pictured in 1980, Prof. Bonita J. Campbell was the first female faculty member in the College of Engineering and Computer Science. She founded the Department of Manufacturing Systems Engineering and Management. In order to foster the development of women in the engineering profession, she created the Bonita J. Campbell Endowment for Women in Science and Engineering (WISE) in collaboration with the Oviatt Library.

The Summer Program for Economically Disadvantaged Youth (SPEDY) was funded by the US Department of Labor to provide summer employment and job training opportunities to American youths. Over the course of the national program, CSUN hosted dozens of participants, generally between the ages of 14 and 21. Seen here in 1977 are employees Wilma Foster (left) and Katrina Fuller of San Fernando.

United Farm Workers president Cesar Chavez spoke on campus in April 1976, a year after his first scheduled appearance was cancelled over speaking fees, sparking a student demonstration. In September of the same year, Chavez returned to continue his effort to register voters and inform them of California Proposition 14, which would have ensured the enforcement of agricultural labor laws. The proposition did not pass.

Folk musician and professor Beth Lomax Hawes (left) is pictured with famed cultural anthropologist and curator Margaret Mead around 1975. The daughter of American folk musicologist John A. Lomax, Hawes joined SFVSC's Anthropology Department in 1968 before taking a position at the Smithsonian Center for Folklife and Cultural Heritage in Washington, DC, where she worked with folklorists from around the world.

Aaron Copland, the highly regarded composer of works such as *Fanfare for the Common Man* and *Appalachian Spring*, helped define the sound of Americana in a genre dominated by European and Russian composers. On May 6, 1975, CSUN held a music festival honoring the composer in which he conducted students in a concert of many of his works. Copland (left) is seen here during rehearsal with Prof. David Whitwell.

At age 82, world-renowned Spanish classical guitarist Andrés Segovia visited the acclaimed CSUN guitar program led by Prof. Ron Purcell in 1976. The intimate classroom setting was filled with enthusiastic students, some of whom had the honor of performing for the maestro, who graciously worked with the young performers. At the event, George Vick performed *Homenaje: Le Tombeau de Debussy*, by composer Manuel de Falla.

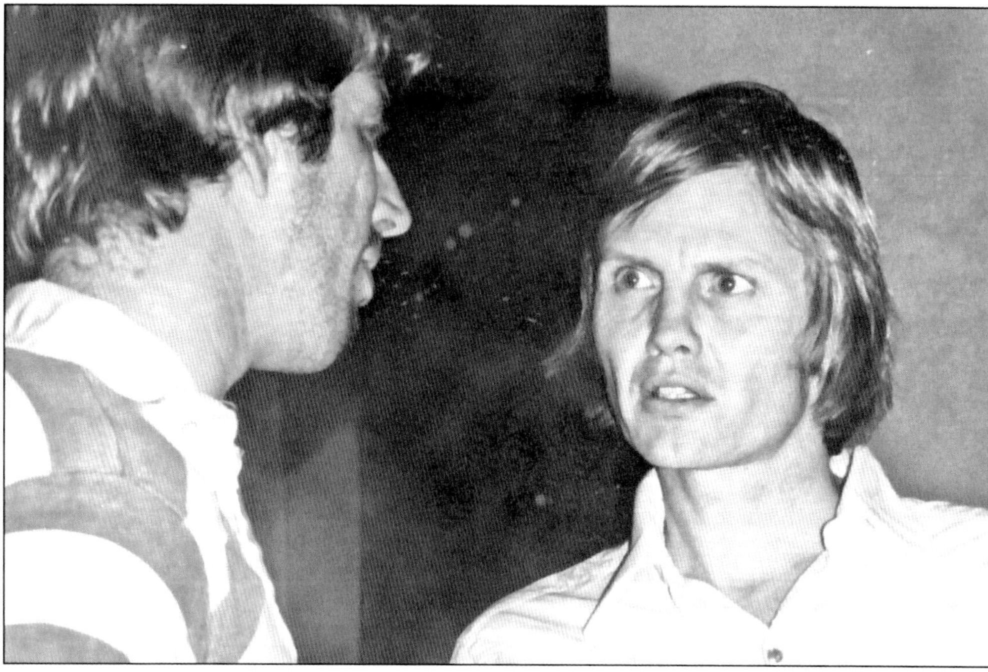

In 1976, actor Jon Voight (right), star of *Midnight Cowboy* (1969) and *Deliverance* (1972), played the lead in the Theatre Department production of *Hamlet*. Such events gave students exceptional access to industry professionals, as seen in this rehearsal photograph. The play featured CSUN theater student Terry Hins as Claudius (left) and ran from March 3 to March 13, 1976, at the Campus Theatre.

Actor, writer, and director Charles Martin Smith is pictured with actress Cindy Dunbar at a fundraising reception in 1980 presented by the CSUN Arts Council. The performances raised money to establish a scholarship fund for the Theatre Department. Smith, a CSUN alumnus, starred as Terry the Toad in *American Graffiti* (1973) while still a junior. He went on to star in such other critically acclaimed films as *Starman* (1984) and *The Untouchables* (1987).

Since the production of a sound stage in the drama and speech department in 1961, CSUN has been noted for its bold innovations in film arts education. CSUN is now recognized among the world's elite film schools. The Department of Cinema and Television Arts consistently places numerous professionals within all areas of the film and television industry. In these c. 1980 photographs, an instructor orients the class to the camera equipment (above) in preparation for filming a subject (below).

Like many of the nation's youth in the 1960s and 1970s, CSUN students sought to apply their skills and make a difference by entering the Peace Corps. Alumnus Frank Casey traveled to Mouit, Senegal, in 1973 to assist people in the Fleuve region who struggled under six years of drought. The production of wells, as seen here, helped move farmers from subsistence farming to income-producing crops.

As in many classrooms, learning by doing is a popular approach to teaching scientific phenomena. In this c. 1975 photograph, a student demonstrates electrostatic conduction using a Van de Graaff generator. Once touched, the electricity trapped within the cylinder is conducted through the dome to the student volunteer, causing her hair to lift from her head due to imbalanced electrical charges.

Geomorphology is the study of the origin and evolution of land formations. Sedimentology is the study of the creation, movement, and distribution of land sediments such as sand, clay, and silt. As branches of earth science, these two areas of study are demonstrated through this river model around 1975. Students analyze both erosion and deposition through the natural movement of water across the platform over time.

By 1980, CSUN was one of six California State University campuses in the Southern California Ocean Studies Consortium. Students across the campuses had access to the *Nautilus*, a 52-foot vessel first launched from Puget Sound in 1946 and later converted to be a research vessel. The *Nautilus* and a smaller vessel provided the impetus for developing support facilities, including labs and lecture rooms at the port of Long Beach.

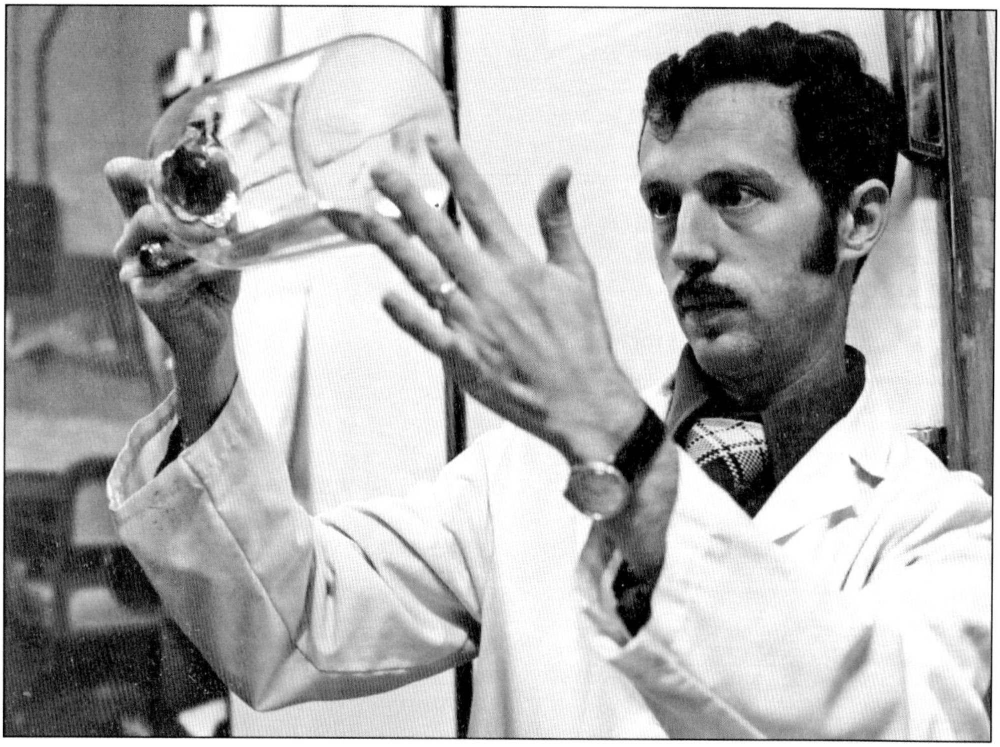

Biology professor and director of the CSUN School of Science and Mathematics Dr. Steven Oppenheimer is pictured in his laboratory in 1991. With assistance from many student coauthors, Oppenheimer produced over 200 articles, abstracts, presentations, and books. Now a professor emeritus, he is a CSU System Trustees Outstanding Professor and received the US Presidential Award from Pres. Barack Obama in 2010.

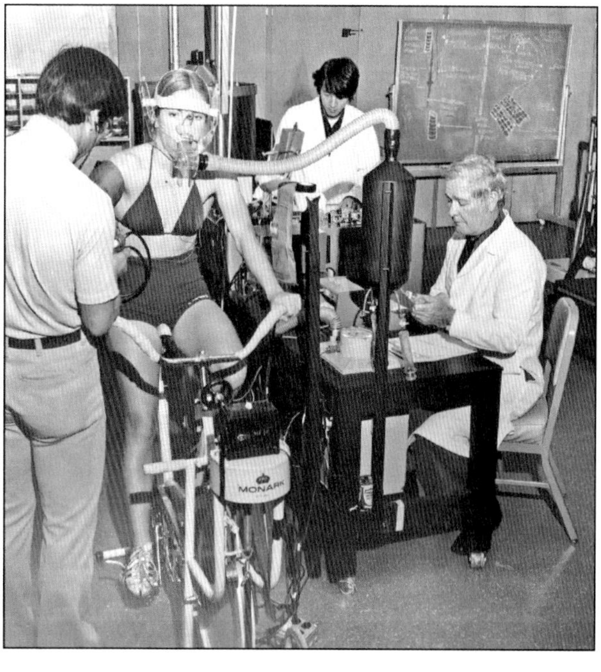

A woman athlete has her blood pressure and respiration rate measured in the Human Performance Laboratory on campus by Dr. George Q. Rich, professor of physical education. Thirty-four women athletes participated in his 1976 study, which ultimately revealed that an athlete's heart function, metabolism, and flexibility improved as a result of participation in competitive sports on campus.

Four

Innovation and Realization 1981–1993

In the 1980s and early 1990s, CSUN continued to grow and change in some ways, while maturing and settling into itself in others. Ever-expanding numbers of faculty and students made use of research facilities around Los Angeles. Faculty research also took place on campus, especially work focused on physical education, disability services, and botany, as faculty and students used the newly created Botanic Garden as a tool for research and teaching. The steadily increasing student body also made for larger and larger commencement ceremonies at the conclusion of each academic year.

To address challenges caused by the growing student population, President Cleary continued working to increase the capacity of campus infrastructure. He planned the development of land to the north of campus at the site of the Devonshire Downs racetrack. It would ultimately include athletic fields, additional on-campus housing, food service, parking, and more. To accommodate the growing number of library resources housed in an already-constructed building, the campus installed an automated storage and retrieval system for books and other resources that dramatically increased the library's storage capacity. Associated Students also made contributions to the development of the campus by funding the construction of the Sierra Tower clock.

Student life outside of the classroom also acquired a unique character in these years. While Greek organizations had been unpopular on campus during the Vietnam era, they became increasingly popular and well established in the 1980s, as did the campus's athletic programs and associated trappings, including cheerleading, the marching band, and more. The EOP established the Summer Bridge Program, which still works to provide academically at-risk students with the tools they need to succeed at CSUN. Evidence of a continuing culture of student activism can be seen in protest actions organized in the wake of proposed fee hikes during the budget crisis of the early 1990s, during the 1992 Los Angeles riots, and more.

When Prof. William Freeman asked students in his speech-communications class to come up with a meaningful campus project, student Elizabeth Haines responded with the idea of installing a clock on the top of Sierra Tower. The Student Projects Committee, led by AS president David Bunker, funded the clock. Bunker lauded Haines's idea as something especially useful to the growing number of deaf students on campus who could not hear the Administration Building's chimes at the start of each new hour. Installation of the east-facing clock cost $4,930. There was money remaining in the fund that was applied to install a second, north-facing clock. The clocks were officially started in a ceremony on October 1, 1983, led by President Cleary as part of CSUN's Silver Anniversary celebration.

For decades, the reflecting pool was a campus landmark. It was installed in 1968 after an anonymous 1963 donation of American Home Products stocks. In the late 1980s, students found a Corvette abandoned in the pool after a police chase. Heavy drought in the early 1990s forced it to be drained and disassembled. Here, the reflecting pool is framed by the Administration Building and the library around 1980.

As part of his plan for excellence, President Cleary and other campus officials envisioned the development of the panhandle north of the main campus, which included athletic fields, housing, and other facilities for a growing student body. The 1987 ground breaking was attended by Los Angeles mayor Tom Bradley. Rincon Hall, visible in the background, was later demolished following the Northridge earthquake.

In 1992, Pres. Blenda Wilson, seen here with sign-language interpreter, presided over the ground-breaking ceremony for expansion of the 30-year-old College of Engineering and Computer Science. The 73,000-square-foot addition was, according to Wilson, a partnership between the California State University system and private donors. Among the supporters was the Rocketdyne division of the Rockwell International Corporation. The addition was completed in September 1994.

Sometimes referred to as the "worm" or "spaghetti" sign, the CSUN sign is seen here from the north in 1992, eighteen years after its completion by artist John Banks. See page 48 to view the sign as it appears facing west. The sign continues to be one of the campus's most photographed landmarks.

The Oviatt Library's Automated Storage and Retrieval System (ASRS) was built as part of an approximately 96,000-square-foot expansion to the library, which also included the addition of two new wings. Dedicated on October 25, 1991, the ASRS uses a system of small cranes that retrieve over 13,000 steel bins containing books, periodicals, and other library materials requested by students and faculty.

Two students care for plants in CSUN's Botanic Garden, located between the University Student Union and Chaparral Hall. Created in 1959, the garden contains over 1,000 plant species, including cacti, succulents, tropical plants, California natives, palms, herbs, and more. It is a valuable resource for students and faculty interested in plant biology, ecology, morphology, and physiology, as well as entomology, and also serves the broader community.

In 1986, the Ocean Studies Research Consortium purchased a Hawaiian albacore tuna vessel in order to coordinate activities between the marine biology, marine geology, and ocean engineering programs of the CSU system. The vessel, renamed *Yellowfin*, replaced the *Nautilus* and ensured that CSU students could continue to conduct marine research. In this 1987 photograph, CSUN students and crew idle off the coast of Manhattan Beach.

Dr. Sam Britten, professor of physical education, pioneered CSUN's adaptive physical education plan. While the program was originally designed to assist students recovering from injuries, it eventually grew to include physical education for the disabled. Here he demonstrates exercises to a group of disabled students on campus in May 1984.

CSUN students walk up a spiral staircase in the 1980s to view the 24-inch coudé telescope at the San Fernando Observatory, a solar research facility in Sylmar that is affiliated with CSUN. The telescope's unique design allows observers using it to remain in one place while the telescope follows the sun's path across the sky.

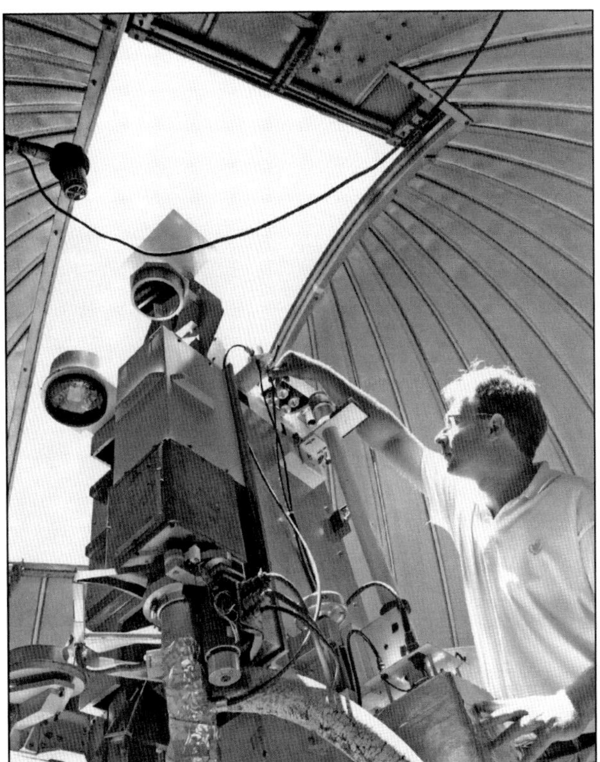

In the 1980s, a man operates the coudé telescope at the San Fernando Observatory. Telescope operators could study the sun's image in detail directly through the telescope's eyepiece or on a small television screen. A spectroheliograph attached to the telescope could be used to take photographs of the sun at different wavelengths.

For a time, CSUN enjoyed highly competitive and successful men's and women's fencing teams, even producing an All-American fencer in Karl Dempwork in 1963. The fencing tradition carried on into the 1980s, as seen in this match between CSUN student Janna Hunt (right) and her opponent from California State University, Fullerton.

In 1981 and 1982, local resident Dave Knudsen worked to bring wheelchair basketball to CSUN. The Physical Therapy Club scheduled games and sold tickets, most often as fundraisers for charities that supported the disabled. Matches were sometimes against opponents like the Whittier Wings, then the third-ranked wheelchair basketball team in California.

CSUN cheerleaders are pictured in formation at a homecoming pep rally on the Oviatt lawn in 1988 as members of the football team watch from the side and students peer down from the portico with banners, signs, and balloons. Absent from the image are the Oviatt Library stairs, which were constructed in 2000.

CSUN's Matador Marching Band performs during halftime at a football game on campus in uniforms funded by a loan from Associated Students in 1982. Beyond supporting the Matador football and basketball teams throughout the year, the band also marched in numerous professional and college sporting events through the 1980s, including the 99th Annual Tournament of Roses in Pasadena and Super Bowl XXII at Jack Murphy Stadium in San Diego.

Members of the Phi Kappa Alpha fraternity and Delta Delta Delta sorority pose with roller skates and a skateboard in front of their partially completed homecoming float in the mid-1980s. In 1985, campus officials judged roller skates and skateboards to be the cause of a number of pedestrian injuries on campus and began enforcing no-tolerance bans of both.

Members of Phi Beta Sigma's Kappa Alpha chapter pose for a photograph. Formed in 1978, the chapter engages deeply in the community, participating in and helping to organize service events around campus including blood drives, voter registration programs, sickle cell disease research, feeding the homeless, and providing workshops for African American men on campus.

As part of Greek Week activities in 1984, fraternities participated in a keg tossing competition. Greek Week, an event designed to unite Greeks and help them fulfill their philanthropic duties, had participation from all Greek organizations on campus for the first time that year. The event's theme was "CSUN Greeks, unofficial sponsors for the 1984 Olympics."

Members of fraternities and sororities participate in a tug-of-war on the Oviatt lawn in the mid-1980s as part of the Matador Madness Olympiad. The event featured races through an obstacle course, a balloon toss, and a game of earthball as a part of the annual homecoming celebration, which also included the All-University Party, pep rallies, parades, and the crowning of the homecoming king and queen.

Members of CSUN's Epsilon Xi chapter of the Kappa Kappa Gamma sorority pose for a photograph during an event on campus in the early 1980s. Founded in 1974, CSUN's chapter emphasizes academic success, philanthropy, and community service, focusing its attention on philanthropy and community involvement both on and off campus.

Members of CSUN's Sigma Phi chapter of the Alpha Omicron Pi sorority pose for a photograph around 1988. Seen as part of the establishment, fraternities and sororities were unpopular on campus during the Vietnam era, with many Greek organizations folding. Despite being installed in 1967, Alpha Omicron Pi survived, gaining in popularity through the 1980s. It continues to thrive.

Members of CSUN's Epsilon Phi chapter of the Sigma Gamma Rho sorority pose for a formal photograph in the early 1980s. Established in 1973, as opportunities in higher education became more widely available to more Americans, the Epsilon Phi chapter of the Sigma Gamma Rho sorority has served as a support system for women students at CSUN for several decades.

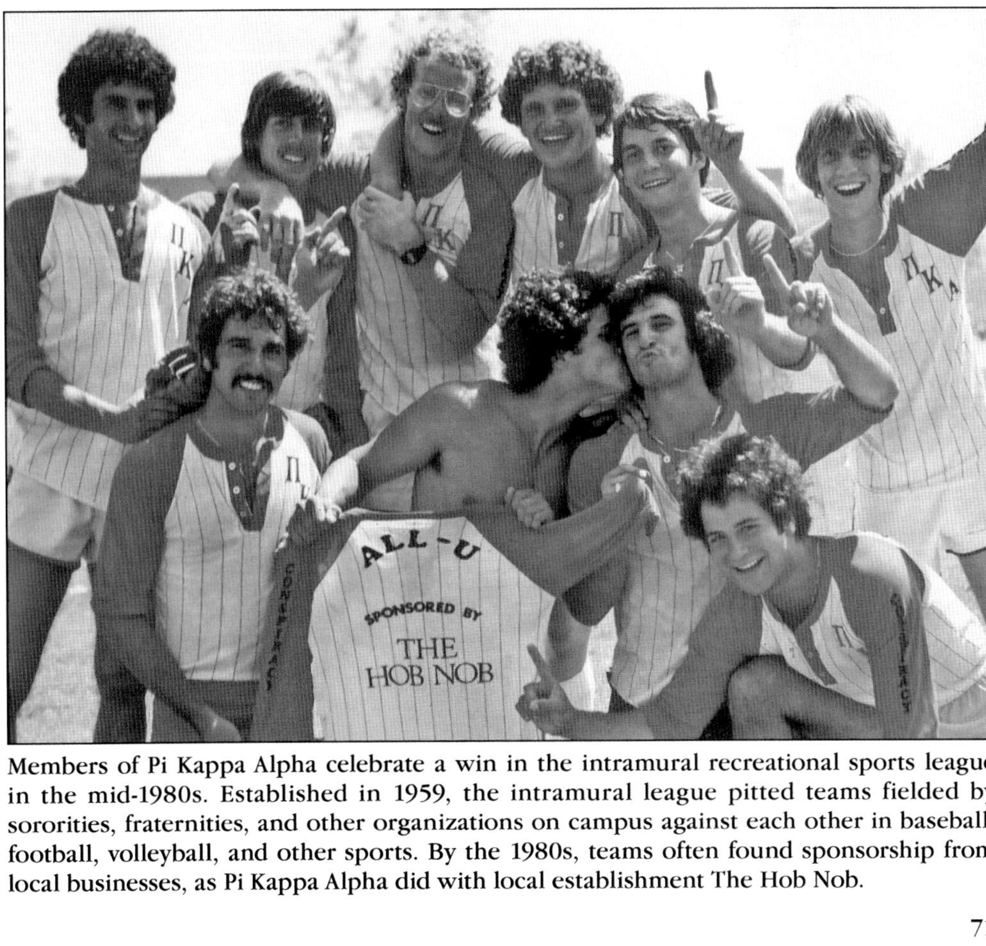

Members of Pi Kappa Alpha celebrate a win in the intramural recreational sports league in the mid-1980s. Established in 1959, the intramural league pitted teams fielded by sororities, fraternities, and other organizations on campus against each other in baseball, football, volleyball, and other sports. By the 1980s, teams often found sponsorship from local businesses, as Pi Kappa Alpha did with local establishment The Hob Nob.

When the CSU Board of Trustees approved Gov. Pete Wilson's proposal to raise student fees in the CSU system by 40 percent, student members of Movimiento Estudiantil Chicanx de Aztlán (MEChA) led over 300 students in a protest march from the University Student Union to the Oviatt lawn on March 18, 1992. Several clubs and organizations cosponsored the event, with students wearing yellow armbands acting as security to ensure that the protest remained orderly.

Students and faculty protested racism and called for an integrated, multiethnic curriculum on campus at a teach-in on the Oviatt lawn after the Los Angeles riots in 1992. Organized by the BSU, campus administration, and AS, over 200 people listened to speakers discuss their opinions on the not-guilty verdicts in the trial of four Los Angeles police officers who beat Rodney King.

The Summer Bridge Program is an extended orientation that provides help for new students transitioning to university life. The multiweek program provides social and academic benefits, with many activities and workshops designed to build skills necessary for collegiate success. Students are admitted based on need, and the program has consistently given them confidence as they enter the university. In 1988, over 200 freshmen and 100 transfer students participated.

Mayor Tom Bradley makes an unexpected visit to CSUN on September 15, 1988, to declare the establishment of National Deaf Awareness Week. Then-director of the National Center on Deafness (NCOD) Herb Larson led the mayor on a tour of the NCOD facility. The visit also included a brief question-and-answer period with hearing-impaired students.

Chemistry graduates show their pride by holding up placards during commencement exercises on May 22, 1981. Over 2,500 graduates accepted diplomas on the Oviatt lawn that day before a crowd of approximately 15,000 guests. During his remarks, President Cleary described the assembled graduates as "festive" and said their "processional horseplay and reactive body language" were signs of a class of "evolved achievers and winsome winners."

CSUN has been a popular commuter campus for those seeking new careers or looking to quench a lifelong desire to earn an elusive college degree. In 1991, Katherine Chamlis graduated with a degree in English at the age of 82. A member of the 1932 graduating class of Gardena High School, the Lancaster resident traveled 60 miles to and from campus twice a week with a professor.

Wearing his full academic regalia, CSUN president James Cleary shakes hands with each newly hooded graduate of a master's program in the College of Education on the Oviatt lawn in 1987. At the conclusion of the ceremony, new graduates switched their tassels from right to left, thus signifying they had received their diplomas.

By 1989, the size of the student population stressed the graduation ceremony held on campus. In an attempt to address the problem, CSUN held its commencement at the Hollywood Bowl. Initially, the ceremony was scheduled to begin at 7:00 a.m. in order to continue the tradition of a dawn commencement. Students protested, and the time was moved back to 11:00 a.m. to accommodate departmental receptions on campus.

In 1990, political activist and former UCLA professor of philosophy Angela Davis spoke to an enthusiastic crowd of students in the University Student Union for Black History Month. Davis challenged students to confront the inequality of blacks and women, encouraging them to be self-reliant as activists. Students attending the speech credited her as an inspiring and motivating influence in their lives.

British American actor John Houseman, best known as Charles W. Kingsfield in the movie and television series *The Paper Chase*, spoke to an audience of approximately 400 in San Fernando Valley Hall in October 1983. Houseman's portrayal of Kingsfield won him an Academy Award in 1973. His character was inspired by an actual Harvard Law School professor known for his intimidating intellectual assaults on his students.

Five

Rebuilding a Campus Community 1994–2009

At 4:30 a.m. on January 17, 1994, a 6.7-magnitude earthquake struck the San Fernando Valley. While the early-morning hour and Martin Luther King Jr. holiday meant campus buildings were unoccupied during the event, many lives were lost in the surrounding community. The damage left in the quake's wake was catastrophic across Southern California but especially so in the valley and on campus. The CSUN community mobilized in the earthquake's immediate aftermath, with some individuals focusing on campus relief efforts before personal ones. In a great show of determination and perseverance, students, faculty, and administrators started classes for the spring 1994 semester only two weeks late. They worked out of tents, trailers, and other temporary structures as emergency and construction crews began rebuilding critical infrastructure. While the recovery process was prolonged, the earthquake and its aftermath altered not only the physical appearance of the campus but also its culture.

CSUN served as a hub and resource for the surrounding community in the earthquake's aftermath and continued in this role after recovery efforts had largely ceased. Numerous exhibitions and events staged in the campus art galleries attracted visitors from across Los Angeles, and in 2008, the campus broke ground for a new performing arts center in the valley. It also continued to play host to important guests like Maya Angelou, Huell Howser, and Dolores Huerta, as well as politicians, including 2008 Democratic presidential candidate Hillary Clinton, Senators Barbara Boxer and Dianne Feinstein, and Gov. Arnold Schwarzenegger.

As CSUN approached and celebrated its 50th anniversary with a series of special events and exhibitions in 2008, its shape and form continued to change. Major renovations to the USU were completed in 2006. Student services also continued to expand, with the opening of the Veterans Resource Center, the Pride Center, and other support programs. Student activism continued to be a regular part of campus life, with student groups organizing demonstrations, marches, and other protest actions in response to Sacramento's proposal to increase tuition 10 percent across the CSU system, US military actions in Afghanistan, and more.

Parking structures across campus sustained severe damage during the January 17, 1994, Northridge earthquake. Many interstates, including the 5 and 10, buckled or collapsed, and over 70 fires erupted from ruptured gas lines. Members of the local community filled campus lawns and parking lots with tents, grills, and sleeping bags that afternoon and evening as students, faculty, and neighbors of CSUN left their homes fearing aftershocks and further destruction to houses and apartments.

During the 1994 earthquake, the Science 4 Building suffered structural and cosmetic damage, while the Science 1, 2, and 3 Buildings caught on fire. Fears of chemical, biological, and radioactive toxicity challenged emergency responders from 17 firefighting companies and a hazardous materials unit, who worked to safely extinguish the fires and rescue nearly 100 mice in the basement of one of the buildings.

Some of the most severe damage to the Oviatt Library during the earthquake occurred on the north side of the building, where windows lined the external walls of the core and wings. Though the columns remained largely intact, the extended roofing they supported gave way in several locations between columns. Damage to the library's exterior was serious, but its core was declared structurally stable in the days after the quake. Inside the building, library shelving had been braced and reinforced before the disaster and survived the earthquake undamaged. Even so, over a million books and other library materials were thrown to the floor on all four levels of the building. The violent shaking even dislodged call number signs at the end of each row of shelves, providing further evidence of the extraordinary forces involved.

Campus security officer Daryl Boid guards the perimeter of a campus parking structure at the corner of Zelzah Avenue and Plummer Street in the days immediately following the 1994 Northridge earthquake. The structure, which became symbolic of the truly remarkable damage that can occur in a seismic event, was located about three kilometers from the quake's epicenter. It was ultimately slated for demolition and replaced with tennis courts.

CSUN administration moved into temporary trailers labeled "Executive Offices" in the Northridge earthquake's aftermath. Many colleges and universities in Southern California offered their assistance through donations of clothing, supplies, and labor for cleanup. A special "earthquake edition" of the *Daily Sundial* that featured tributes to students and other members of the CSUN community killed in the disaster also contained a letter to the campus community from Pres. Blenda Wilson.

A crane positioned in front of the Oviatt Library's original west wing is reflected in a pool of water in the foreground months after the January 1994 Northridge earthquake. The core of the library was constructed in 1973 and contained reinforced concrete, which remained structurally intact. The building's wings, however, were completed just three years prior to the disaster using steel frame reinforcements from the foundation through the fourth floor. Four-inch steel base plates that supported the frame cracked under the stress of the shaking. Despite these measures intended to improve the structural integrity of the building during earthquakes, the east and west wings of the library ultimately suffered irreparable damage, requiring that they be fenced off, demolished, and rebuilt. Six years after the disaster, repairs were finally completed, and the library reopened to full service for the fall 2000 semester.

The CSUN community worked quickly and efficiently in an effort to restore the campus in time for the spring 1994 semester. Temporary signs were posted across campus in late January, and ads were included in a special earthquake edition of the *Daily Sundial* that included a phone number students and others could call for information about the situation.

In the earthquake's violent shaking, millions of books in the Oviatt Library were thrown to the floor in heaps and piles. The building itself, a concrete structure built in the early 1970s, was also damaged in the earthquake, but its core was restored for service in time for the fall 1994 semester.

Though construction crews and volunteers worked diligently to get the campus up and running as quickly as possible, significant damage was still visible as classes started in temporary trailers and tents on February 14, four weeks after the earthquake and two weeks after the previously scheduled first day of classes that term. Hundreds of portable classrooms and structures were said to have been ordered to facilitate the reopening of the campus, with about 35 mobile buildings already in place and functioning within a few weeks of the quake. Though many campus buildings remained open, many were lost, requiring classes to be temporarily moved to local high schools and community colleges throughout the valley and as far south as Los Angeles City College and UCLA. Provost Louanne Kennedy announced that the two-week delay would be compensated by the removal of spring break and the postponement of graduations to June 7–9. In an attempt to build morale during this difficult time, campus public relations developed the motto "Not just back . . . Better!", which met with mixed reactions among those heavily burdened by the new circumstances.

Commemorating the one-year anniversary of the 1994 Northridge earthquake, Pres. Bill Clinton spoke in front of the Oviatt Library on January 17, 1995, while standing in front of a year-old image of a collapsed parking structure on campus. In front of the large crowd, Clinton stated, "I said that we wouldn't let you pick up the pieces alone, that we would stay on until the job is done. Twenty-seven federal agencies worked with state and local officials in unprecedented ways and this was the most efficient and effective disaster operation in American history. CSUN is a symbol of the ability of the people of this state to keep coming back following adversity after adversity." Also in attendance at the event were Lt. Gov. Gray Davis, mayor of Los Angeles Richard Riordan, and CSUN president Blenda Wilson.

In CSUN's first presidential visit, President Clinton is greeted by students and others as he arrives on campus in January 1995. Clinton and those greeting him stand where the Oviatt stairs were later built. Cranes and other evidence of the campus's multimillion-dollar rebuilding effort can be seen in the background.

The Oviatt and South Libraries suffered severe damage during the earthquake and were both closed for repair. In May, the campus opened the 15,000-square-foot Lindley Library Dome as a temporary study area and storage for library books and other materials. Pierce College, Mission College, the University of Southern California, and others offered full library services to CSUN students. UCLA held CSUN library materials during the rebuilding period.

In 2005, the CSUN Main Gallery featured an exhibition of Chicano art including a mixture of media such as paintings, jewelry, installations, technology, and an automobile. The exhibit, titled Mirando al Sur/Miranda al Norte, featured the works of 54 artists. It was co-curated by journalism professor Kent Kirkton and East Los Angeles College professor Sybil Venegas.

Actor and director Richard "Cheech" Marin, an avid collector of Chicana/o art, presented the exhibition The Chicano Collection/La Colleción Chicana at the art department's main gallery in 2006. The exhibit featured 27 artists, including Gilbert Luhan, Margaret Garcia, David Botello, and Artemio Rodriguez. Marin, a 1978 graduate of CSUN and 2004 recipient of the Distinguished Alumni Award, is seen here with art professors Louise Lewis and David Moon.

Huell Howser, the host of the PBS television show *California's Gold*, spoke at the Oviatt Library in 2008 to kick off the exhibit Wish You Were Here: Travelers from Antiquity to Modern Times. His presence was particularly meaningful given his travels around California for over two decades exposing to TV viewers the undiscovered treasures and people of the state. A native of Tennessee, Howser's career in California began as a feature journalist for CBS before he ventured out to produce and star in his show, which is adored by Californians everywhere. In this photograph, Howser chats with fans inside the Oviatt Library's exhibit gallery.

On September 11, 2002, the one-year anniversary of Osama Bin Laden's attack on the World Trade Center, a group of faculty, students, and community members joined to participate in an antiwar protest and teach-in that included a silent march and open-mic forum. The event was organized by MEChA, the BSU, the Central American United Students Association, and the CSUN Greens, who formed a joint antiwar group called Students Against War. After assembling on the Oviatt lawn, participants marched through Jerome Richfield and Sierra Halls and around the science and business buildings with banners and signs. They circled back to the Oviatt for a teach-in, where individuals had the opportunity to speak against the war in Afghanistan and the impending Iraq war, which would begin in March of the following year. (Both, Rodolfo F. Acuña Collection.)

In 2002, while serving as the keynote speaker for the College of Humanities graduation, Dolores Huerta received an honorary doctorate degree from Pres. Jolene Koester and Chicana/o studies professor Jorge Garcia. Huerta founded the Agricultural Workers Association (AWA) and later cofounded the United Farm Workers Association with Cesar Chavez in 1962. For decades, Huerta has been a frequent campus speaker, addressing and inspiring students over such issues as the fair housing Proposition 14 (1976), the antidiscrimination Proposition 209 (1996), and women's rights (1998 and 1999).

Maya Angelou addresses a crowd of 2,300 students and faculty at the Matadome during a campus visit in 2009. She opened by singing an excerpt from a 19th-century slave song and described the campus as "a rainbow in the clouds." Students who won an essay contest sponsored by the USU prior to her visit were able to meet Angelou in person before the lecture.

Sen. Barbara Boxer visited campus on October 29, 2010, at the invitation of the CSUN Young Democrats for a campaign rally in the final days of her last senatorial race. Boxer, who was introduced by Sen. Dianne Feinstein, hoped to persuade students to vote in the upcoming election and to explain the differences between herself and her opponent in the race, Republican Carly Fiorina.

CSUN and community leaders joined in the Mike Curb College Courtyard on April 30, 2008, to officially break ground for what was then called the Valley Performing Arts Center (later renamed the Soraya). After a fanfare from the CSUN Brass Ensemble, curtains opened to reveal a bulldozer that dropped a pile of dirt beside the stage. CSUN president Jolene Koester, some Los Angeles City Council members, and donors donned hard hats and ceremonially dug into the pile. Film director and producer Gary Marshall was the master of ceremonies. The center's design was led by Jamie Milne Rojek of HGA Architects and Engineers, who explained to the crowd of approximately 500 that the 1,700-seat venue would accommodate a variety of performing art, from music to theater to movie premieres.

In February 2008, Gov. Arnold Schwarzenegger visited CSUN accompanied by his wife, Maria Shriver (right). After planned student fee hikes were frozen in 2006, subsequent economic hardships for the state led to a reversal, causing steep reductions in state educational support and a proposed 10-percent raise in tuition. As a result, CSUN students formed the coalition known as Students Together Against Raising Tuition (START). As the governor gave his speech in a campus performance hall, a small but enthusiastic crowd of students protested the increase in student fees and cuts to financial aid outside.

In 2008, Sen. Hillary Rodham Clinton of New York ran in the Democratic presidential primary. Her campaign rented the USU's Grand Salon for an event in January of that year, where Clinton, introduced by Los Angeles mayor Antonio Villaraigosa, held a town hall–style meeting with CSUN students and others. With members of the Secret Service on campus to protect the former first lady, over 2,000 attendees watched on monitors in the Plaza del Sol after the Grand Salon filled to capacity. The crowd's biggest response came when Clinton promised to end the abuses of student loan companies, improve the Pell Grant system, and do away with confusing federal student loan forms.

CSUN celebrated its 50th anniversary in 2008. The celebration was officially titled 50 Years of Life-Changing Opportunity and included special events, exhibitions, an anniversary website featuring an interactive timeline, and many other activities. In honor of the 50-year milestone, the first annual Founders' Day was instituted to commemorate the school's past. The festivities in 2008 included events for some of the first students at the campus, known as the 50-Year Club, who traveled from across the country for the grand reunion. Throughout the academic year, the campus was decorated with over 200 red, white, and black banners that greeted students, faculty, and visitors.

In 2008, CSUN president Jolene Koester, archivist Robert G. Marshall (kneeling), and others opened a time capsule that had been sealed for 25 years beneath the small sundial at the southwest corner of the Oviatt Library. Sealed in October 1983, the time capsule contained messages written to the future CSUN community, reflective pieces about CSUN in 1983, and a survey of faculty, administrators, and student leaders that had been conducted by professors Gail Fonosch and Earl Bogdanoff. Drs. Fonosch and Bogdanoff also included a copy of the design for the computer system used to conduct the survey, as they predicted significant technological advances would occur by 2008. The time capsule's contents were featured in an exhibition in the Oviatt Library titled Fifty and Fabulous.

Students, faculty, and staff protested a new round of cuts to the CSU system proposed by Governor Schwarzenegger in 2008. The mid-year cut of $66 million helped drive up the cost of tuition for hundreds of thousands of CSU students and effectively froze salaries for faculty and staff across the system. It compounded the pressure brought through steep reductions in the CSU operating budget for 2008–2009, which was $250 million below operating requirements before the mid-year cut was announced. The cut was just one in a string of devastating educational funding reductions dating back to the previous five years, sparking heightened levels of outrage by those affected most.

On March 4, 2010, CSUN students and faculty participated in a statewide Day of Action to protest budget cuts to the CSU system. Several professors cancelled classes, and many students walked out to participate in the protest. Students and others gathered in numerous locations around campus, including the Oviatt lawn, and marched down Reseda Boulevard. Four CSUN students were arrested during the protest activities. Five days after the walkout, faculty and students gathered to voice concerns over injurious treatment at the hands of police officers and issued demands that included the dismissal of charges and citations filed during the protest. The city offered to drop all misdemeanor charges except for one. However, in an act of solidarity, the students collectively refused.

The University Student Union, known as the USU, underwent major renovations costing $15 million in the early 2000s. Despite significant delays caused by unusually inclement weather, phase two of the renovations concluded just before the fall 2006 term began. The campus held a grand reopening celebration for the improved USU in August of that year.

In Hurricane Katrina's aftermath, the CSUN community launched a relief campaign that aimed to raise $500,000. Provost Harry Hellenbrand's messages about the effort emphasized its importance given the strong support and assistance CSUN received after the 1994 Northridge earthquake. Many campus groups made donations or organized fundraising events, including Associated Students, the men's basketball team, the Alpha Phi Alpha fraternity, and others.

Six

Looking Forward 2010–Present

Today, faculty and the broader campus community work hard to support students. This support ranges from organization and promotion of the annual AppJam, CSUNposium, and other student research initiatives, to mentoring and other kinds of one-on-one engagement. Commencement ceremonies now run over the course of several days. More broadly, a growing culture of engagement and giving on campus has emerged not only from students, faculty, and administrators who remembered the significant support received by CSUN in the earthquake's aftermath, but also from alumni and other philanthropists who have donated their time, money, and other resources to help support CSUN students and the broader community.

Student life today resembles that of any other time in some ways but is also unique and distinct. With the average age of CSUN students lowering with each passing year, today's students participate in events organized by the campus and Associated Students such as the Big Show, Matador Nights, and GradFest. Activism continues to be a major component of campus culture, with students organizing demonstrations around the anniversary of the Armenian genocide, proposed budget cuts to the CSU system, and an enrollment freeze on campus that occurred as a result of a state-wide budget crisis.

In just a handful of decades, hundreds of thousands of students have attended and graduated from CSUN. While a few faculty members on loan from Cal State Los Angeles taught CSUN's first students in classrooms at San Fernando High School, today over 2,000 faculty members serve 40,000 students pursuing bachelor's degrees in 69 disciplines, master's degrees in 58 fields, doctorates in two fields, and 14 teaching credential programs. Though still relatively young, CSUN has developed a distinct and prized campus culture. Beyond providing an education, faculty and administrators work to help students find their voices and think critically about their role in communities both on and off campus.

In the 1990s, plans to add a statue of the campus mascot led the art department to hold a design competition. All plans were dropped in the earthquake's aftermath, but in 2008, they were revived. A nationwide contest ensued as Associated Students allocated the initial $10,000 needed for the statue. The bronze statue is seen nearly finished in 2010.

Though some students objected to Associated Students' allocation of $10,000 for the matador statue amidst the budget crisis that followed the 2008 financial crisis, significant alumni contributions helped sculptor Jon Hair begin work on the project, which cost $150,000. The seven-foot matador statue was installed in September 2011, in time for Freshman Convocation. In this photograph, Hair guides the statue into place atop its marble base.

Matador Nights is the annual festival for students to kick off the new academic year featuring games, food, and live music. The 2016 festival took a nostalgic look at the 1990s as its central theme, with retro arcade games such as *Tetris* and *Dance Dance Revolution*. Reference to television shows from the decade, such as *Saved by the Bell*, were also on display. The main event of the evening was provided by Mix Master Mike of Beastie Boys fame. In these photographs, a student emerges from a bounce house obstacle course (above), and a group of students gets caught up in the festival excitement (below).

In its final game of the 2016 regular season, CSUN's men's soccer team clinched the Big West championship at home with a 2-1 overtime win against Cal State Fullerton, guaranteeing it a slot in the NCAA Division I championship tournament. Seen here at the Pub Sports Grill (above), the team anxiously awaits the announcement of its seeding and first opponent. The team ultimately faced Pacific in a narrow 0-1 defeat. As tradition mandates, the 2018 Big West women's basketball champions gathered for the announcement of their NCAA Division I fate in the highly competitive national tournament (below). The team lost to Notre Dame.

Student attendees at CSUN's annual Big Show, a multi-artist concert staged each fall, raise their arms as confetti falls from above. Started in 2001 and organized by Associated Students, the Big Show brings in hundreds of thousands of dollars in revenue each year and has featured such artists as Lupe Fiasco, Ludacris, Common, Big Sean, and Diplo, among others.

The Oviatt lawn plays host to a number of student-centered and other events each year. These include the annually recurring Big Show, Associated Students' Summer Movie Fest, Honors Convocation, commencement, and more. Due to its central location on the campus and the size of the lawn itself, it also serves as a popular starting or concluding location for demonstrations, marches, and protest actions.

Dr. William Watkins, vice president for student affairs, looks on as students participate in the Take Class Action sit-in in CSUN's University Hall in protest of ongoing budget cuts to the CSU system. Organized by Students for Quality Education (SQE), the sit-in was one of many protest activities that took place across the CSU and University of California systems with the full support of the California Faculty Association on April 13, 2011.

Just prior to the spring 2012 semester, an organized group of student protesters met on the Oviatt lawn and marched down Cleary Walk past Bayramian Hall before meeting Provost Harry Hellenbrand to discuss their concerns. Provost Hellenbrand answered questions and spoke with students about campus administration's decision to implement an enrollment freeze in University Hall's breezeway.

CSUN's Armenian Students Association (ASA) and the Armenian fraternity Alpha Epsilon Omega engage in a silent and nonviolent demonstration called Stain of Denial on Matador Walk to raise awareness of the Armenian Genocide, which began in 1915. The demonstrations, which occur annually, are organized by ASA and take place concurrently on campuses around the world.

The Chicana/o Studies (CCS) Department celebrated its 45th anniversary in 2014. In April, the USU's Grand Salon hosted a symposium featuring students, CCS faculty, and others. In September, MEChA and other students organized a joint celebration of Chicana/o studies and the EOP featuring music and dancing from the Ballet Folklórico Aztlán de CSUN and Mariachi Aztlan de San Fernando.

In 1992, as part of demands made by the BSU and others regarding unfair racial treatment, a house on Halstead Street that had served as a meeting place for minority students in the 1970s was provided to the Pan-African Studies Department and BSU. In 2017, following two years of grant-funded renovations, the Black House grand reopening ceremony featured speakers including Provost Yi Li, vice president of student affairs William Watkins, and Africana studies professors Theresa White (above, far right) and Cedric Hackett (above, far left). The renovated house features two conference rooms, a computer lab, a film screening room, and cultural art. Below, a student attending the celebration views a Black Panther Party poster featuring founders Bunchy Carter and Huey P. Newton.

Addressing the issue of mass incarceration of minorities, actor Danny Glover spoke to approximately 300 attendees in the USU's Grand Salon during Black History Month in February 2013. The discussion, moderated by Prof. Theresa White, was cohosted by the Pan-African Studies Department (renamed Africana Studies), the BSU, the Department of Cinema and Television Arts, and the Black Alumni Association. Glover joined a panel including former Black Panther Party member Hank Jones and BSU president Brande Hookfin, all of whom participated in a discussion and took audience questions following the screening of the documentary *The House I Live In*, for which Glover was executive producer. The screening of this film, along with another titled *Bring Herman Home*, promoted consciousness and activism regarding political imprisonment and the disproportionate number of incarcerated African Americans in this country.

In 2016, CSU chancellor Timothy White commissioned a study titled "Serving Displaced and Food Insecure Students in the CSU." The study suggested that as many as 8.7 percent of all students in the CSU system were without a permanent residence. Further, more than one in five students were estimated to lack consistent access to sufficient quantities of food. The majority of the students in the study indicated the need for nutritious food outweighed the stigma attached to using pantry services. As a result, donations from the San Fernando Valley Rescue Mission were collected by a pantry sponsored by the Women's Research and Resource Center. A second pantry, seen here with donors and CSUN alumni Tim Belfield and Daphne Roberts, is sponsored by the Office of Student Involvement and Development. The program, which requires nothing other than a student ID to use, is supported by cash and nonperishable donations.

In 2010, student members of CSUN's LGBTA Club and others began petitioning the campus for an LGBTQ resource center on campus. The Pride Center opened in the USU on August 27, 2012, as a place students could get information and support on coming out, receive health information, meet other members of the community, speak with peer mentors, and more. A grand opening celebration was held in September.

Nearly 40 students in the Chicana/o Studies Department worked to create a mural dedicated to Chicana/o studies teachers and faculty members who have died. Attendees at the mural's 2011 opening reception shared stories and memories about those they had lost and posed for photographs in front of the mural, which fills two walls in a classroom in Jerome Richfield Hall.

In May 2013, CSU chancellor Timothy White presented Dianne Harrison with the Presidential Medallion as the university's fifth president. The formal ceremony, called an investiture, was held at the Valley Performing Arts Center (now the Soraya). It bestows honor and authority on the new university president in front of numerous faculty, staff, and administrators. In her address, President Harrison articulated her commitment to the university through the theme "Unlocking Potential, Cultivating Achievement." With her first academic year nearly completed, she laid out several priorities in the face of reduced fiscal support from the state, including a greater emphasis on funded research, innovation in pedagogy, and partnerships with local economic development organizations. During the ceremony, the development of the Harrison Leadership Award was announced. The award would recognize excellence in achievement for a freshman student in the areas of student government, clubs, and organizations.

CSUN's commitment to sustainability is reflected in the installation of multiple photovoltaic sites that reduce the university's reliance on fossil fuels while saving tens of thousands of dollars. These solar farms, scattered around campus, send energy back to the campus power grid. Two parking lots currently deploy panels that also provide shade to cars. Compare this photograph to the same lot from 1964 on page 21.

The Institute for Sustainability, in conjunction with the nonprofit organization Food Forward, invites students, faculty, staff, and others to harvest oranges in the campus orange grove each year. Seen here in 2017, students use extended claws with baskets to pull and catch the falling fruit. The oranges were subsequently donated to hunger programs provided by the Jewish Family Service of Los Angeles and the Valley Food Bank.

The Student Research and Creative Works Symposium, seen here in 2013, is an annual competition featuring oral and poster presentations with which students present and showcase their research. The competition was started in 1994 by the CSUN Psychology Department in partnership with the psychology honor society Psi Chi in order to prepare undergraduates for the research required in graduate programs. Since its inception, the competition has grown to include student representatives across numerous disciplines in all nine academic colleges. Student research is judged by faculty under the criteria of purpose, methodology, interpretation, presentation, and appearance. In 2017, the competition changed its name to CSUNposium. First- and second-place winners receive cash awards. In this photograph, a student presents his research to interested faculty and guests.

The annual AppJam competition provides an opportunity for CSUN students to work with peers while creating mobile applications, or apps, in an entrepreneurial environment. At the AppJam Showcase, undercover judges visit all the teams to try out their apps and rate them, ultimately selecting winners who receive cash and other prizes. The success of AppJam has spawned other annual technology development competitions, such as DataJam and VARJam (virtual or augmented reality). Above, a student explains his mobile software QRuiser, while below, Alec Tejuco demonstrates his application to an interested attendee.

CSUN managed to grow a rainforest with a fuel cell designed in 2009 by students, faculty, and Physical Plant Management (PPM). The 1-megawatt fuel cell plant is the first of its kind to be installed in an academic institution. It recycles waste emissions of water and carbon dioxide to help sustain the subtropical forest. Eight cooling stations distribute the humid air to the 13,000-square-foot forest. Seen here in 2018, the forest is lush along Matador Walk (above) and in less than a decade has cleared the height of the cooling towers (below).

In 2009, the US House of Representatives designated March 14 National Pi Day to promote engagement in mathematics. Pi Day celebrations at CSUN are cosponsored by the Oviatt Library and the Bonita J. Campbell Foundation for Women in Science and Engineering Endowment. The event gives students an opportunity to explore technological exhibits while enjoying helpings of pie. In this photograph, Isis Leininger demonstrates a 3-D printer from the library's Creative Media Studio.

"Building Infrastructure Leading to Diversity, Promoting Opportunities for Diversity in Education and Research" provides both the mission and acronym for BUILD PODER, a program aimed at providing resources to underrepresented undergraduates in biomedical research. Funded by the National Institutes of Health, the program builds partnerships between students at CSUN, community colleges, and research institutions like the University of California campuses in Los Angeles, San Diego, and Irvine. Here, program participants pose before the Oviatt Library.

For decades, CSUN's undergraduate jazz studies program has consistently produced some of the best collegiate jazz ensembles in the United States. Featuring undergraduate musicians exclusively, CSUN's ensembles successfully compete against other nationally recognized programs that contain postgraduate musicians. Under the direction of Joel Leach (1969–1995), followed by CSUN alumnus and bassist Gary Pratt and pianist Matt Harris, the band has won numerous awards from the Pacific Coast Jazz Festival, the Reno Jazz Festival, and the Monterey Next Generation Jazz Festival. In 2013, the Jazz "A" Band received the honor of *DownBeat* magazine's Best Collegiate Large Ensemble. As ambassadors, the jazz ensembles and combos have frequently performed at high school jazz festivals, providing inspiration to young musicians across Southern California. In this photograph, Harris conducts the Jazz "A" Band in concert.

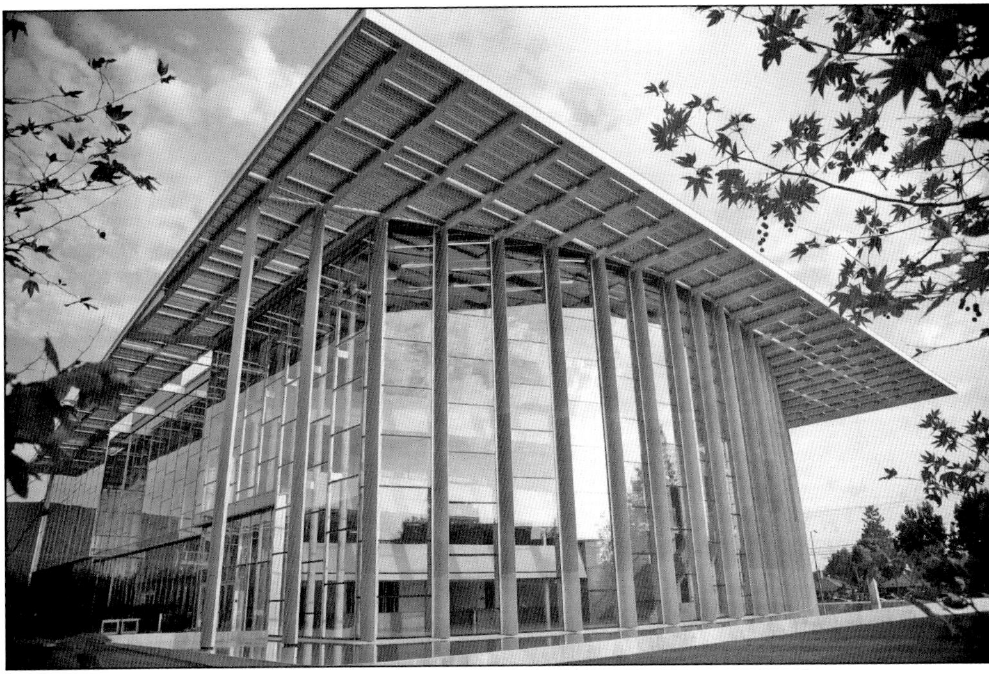

After 10 years of planning and construction, the Valley Performing Arts Center (VPAC) celebrated its grand opening with a gala in 2011 featuring over 20 performers. At a cost of $125 million, the center's lavish exterior is encased almost entirely in glass (above), with the 1,700-seat interior grand hall (below) offering exceptional aesthetics and acoustics through the predominance of natural wood diffusers and surfaces. Almost half the funding for the center came from private donations, including a $2.5-million gift from Clyde and Nancy Porter. In 2017, Los Angeles philanthropists Younes and Soraya Nazarian donated $17 million to the VPAC. The center was formally renamed the Younes and Soraya Nazarian Center for the Performing Arts, often shortened to "the Soraya." The center continues to draw top music and dance performers from around the world.

Among the orange groves surrounding Monterey Hall, CSUN faculty members and others built the University Club, later renamed the Orange Grove Bistro, in 1973 to provide fine dining services to the campus. In 2005, a campus development plan included the construction of a pond, paved walkways, and a stellar observatory within the area. A solar observatory was added in 2014 with a solar charging station. Plans to renovate the bistro and create nearby guest lodging were made in 2018. Pictured here is the entrance to the Orange Grove Bistro. The pond and observatories are accompanied by resident turtles and waterfowl.

CSUN honored former president Blenda Wilson in a courtyard dedication outside the planetarium in 2014. Wilson is noted for her leadership following the 1994 earthquake, student programs like the Presidential Scholars, bolstering opportunities for service learning within CSUN's curricula, and promoting open debates regarding matters of race and affirmative action. She is joined by her Delta Sigma Theta sisters around the courtyard plaque dedicated in her honor.

Every March, graduating seniors, sometimes accompanied by their parents, attend GradFest in the Matador bookstore, which gives students a break from studies to relax and plan for their final act as undergraduates, the commencement ceremony. In shopping for caps, gowns, and other graduation accessories and memorabilia, students become excited as college graduation moves from dream to reality. In this photograph, students pose for senior portraits.

Tens of thousands of students, faculty, and others pass campus landmarks every year, including the Matador Walk and the Ralph Prator Sundial Fountain. The Matador Walk extends from the north side of Sierra Center along the south edge of the Oviatt lawn. One of the main thoroughfares through the central quad, it is the frequent site of tabling by student organizations, demonstrations, and more. The Sundial Fountain was designed in 2000 by a group based out of Carlsbad and modified by PPM. Designers were inspired by the name of the campus newspaper, the *Daily Sundial*. Copper channels control the fountain's water supply, while a computer allows a heavier flow of water to bubble over the Roman numeral representing the time every hour.

Dr. William Watkins is pictured with students participating in a demonstration in support of Deferred Action for Childhood Arrivals, or DACA, in 2016. He first came to CSUN as an undergraduate in the 1970s. In 1973, he became CSUN's first African American president of Associated Students (see page 50). After graduating with a degree in urban studies in 1974, he attended the University of Southern California and the University of California, Los Angeles. His first fulltime staff position at CSUN was as a personal assistant in Human Resources, and he eventually became vice president for student affairs in 2009. Watkins leads numerous offices on campus that contribute to student success and well-being, including University Counseling Services, Disabilities Resources and Educational Services, Financial Aid and Scholarships, the Career Center, Student Housing and Conference Services, and more, in addition to providing administrative oversight to the USU and AS.

Numerous commencement exercises are held on the Oviatt lawn over several days each May. Graduates at every ceremony listen to remarks by the campus president wearing his or her full academic regalia. Here, Dianne Harrison addresses commencement attendees at a ceremony in 2013, her first year as CSUN's president. To the left of the podium is the CSUN mace. Traditionally carried into each commencement ceremony by the dean of the library, the mace symbolizes academic freedom. Since its founding in the 1950s, over 200,000 students have graduated from CSUN with bachelor's and master's degrees in dozens of fields as well as doctoral degrees and special credentials.

Many undergraduates are introduced to formal academic dress for the first time as they prepare for their commencement ceremonies. Some students decorate their mortar boards to help them stand out in the crowd and be more easily spotted by family and friends at the commencement ceremony. With many CSUN students being the first in their families to attend college, mortar board decorations often feature inspirational messages. Commencement exercises bring thousands of friends, family members, and other supporters to campus each May to celebrate and congratulate each year's graduates. The excitement of the ceremony produces lasting memories for all in attendance.

Over the decades since its founding, California State University, Northridge, has experienced growth on a scale that few other academic institutions can claim. The university community has repeatedly confronted great challenges with optimism, perseverance, and humility, celebrating and learning from triumphs and failures. Its success is ultimately built on big thinking from past and present administrators willing

to take chances, faculty who prioritize the needs of all students, and most importantly, students who are unafraid of challenging the status quo. There will be many trials to come, but the CSUN community will ensure this campus continues to provide opportunities for all.

INDEX

About CSUN's University Archives

CSUN's University Archives reside in Special Collections and Archives in the Oviatt Library. They are the home of the historical papers and records of California State University, Northridge, especially its administration, programs, departments, and student life. CSUN's University Archives are a rich resource both for historical research and current administrative needs. Like past university archivists Virginia Ellwood and Robert G. Marshall, university archivist April Feldman works with individuals across campus to collect and provide access to photographs like the ones in this book, documents, and other records of the university's work and activities.

CSUN's University Archives are extensive, containing millions of documents, photographs, and other records. Even so, many of the university's departments and programs are minimally represented or absent. For more information about CSUN's University Archives, including what records are a part of them and what records could yet be transferred, visit library.csun.edu.